THE SQUEAKY WHEEL

COMPLAINING FOR FUN & PROFIT

TOMMIE TITMOUSE

JF

J. FLORES
PUBLICATIONS

P.O. Box 14 Rosemead, CA 91770

ISBN 0-918751-09-8

Library of Congress Catalog Card No. 87-82416

Printed in the United States of America

TABLE OF CONTENTS

INTRODUCTION

OK, so you've been had. Your wallet is flatter than a communion wafer, and the bank played handball with your last check. The credit card machine rejected your last charge, and they locked you out at the local Thrift Shop. The landlord won't fix the faucet, and Friendly Al's Transmission Shop dropped a 1949 Willys Tranny in your '82 Escort. In short, the world's out to get ya, and you're checking your insurance policy for a suicide clause. You've shelled out $149.75 for thirteen different "Revenge" books, but still don't know what to do!

Wait! Listen to me! Sure you can stick pins in a Voodoo Doll or take out phony ads in the local newspaper. But who ya gonna target when you're dealing with some big corporation or a faceless government bureaucracy? Well, my friend, this is why I want you to read this book. During the last 10 years I've taken on a lot of the above, and almost always won. By winning, I mean receiving a nice check in the mail, usually accompanied by a groveling letter of apology. To my way of thinking, the best revenge is money in the ol' hand, the heck with the rest. In the next few chapters I will give you some true case histories (with the names artfully disguised to "protect" the guilty) of how I took on a variety of sloths, sluggards, and just plain old clip artists, and won (and sometimes even made a little extra money in the progress.) So now, boys and girls, let's take a trip down Memory Lane, via little Tommie Titmouse's assorted battles.

CHAPTER 1

THE TELEPHONIC COMPLAINT

The Case Of
The Hungry
Houseguests

Having successfully served my time as a member of Uncle Sam's Armed Forces, protecting our country from Godless Communists (successfully, too, I might add, seen any under your bed lately?), I decided to take advantage of my Veteran's benefits and buy a house, with the loan backed by the Veteran's Administration. Part of the voluminous paperwork required was a Termite Inspection, a certificate stating that the house was inspected by a professional exterminator, and found free of the pesky little critters. This priceless document was provided to me by the attorney at closing, and filed away in my lockbox with various other treasures, such as the clippings from my first haircut and my high school band medals. Fortunate, as it turned out . . .

About 6 weeks after we moved into the house, my wife (who will hereafter be referred to as MW) took me down to the downstairs basement, to show me curious holes in the baseboard of the bathroom, with mud coming out of same, and little white critters who died when exposed to the light. "MW," I said, "I think we got a problem."

The next day I called EZ Kill (remember, all names have been changed) Exterminators, who happened to be close, and offered a "Free Inspection." The inspection was free, but the results were devastating. Termites, I was advised — $640.00 to clean 'em out. OUCH!

After a sleepless night I dug into the old lockbox. We Kill BUGS, Inc. had certified my house as being "clean" just six weeks before. I went for the Yellow Pages and then into action.

Around 10 AM I dialed WKBI and talked to Sally Secretary. In a voice of pain and sorrow, I explained the situation — her firm had given my house a "thumbs up" for termites, six weeks before, and now I had 'em, in spades. She sympathized with me, and transferred me to her supervisor, Charley Gumsmack. In between his smacks (which made me want to reach through the phone lines and throttle him), Charley agreed to send someone out. "I want my people to look, it may just be ants," he glibly told me. "OK," sez I, "Go for it."

The next day we were reinspected. The prognosis was the same — "Queenie" Termite and her children were feasting on my downstairs bathroom. "So what are you going to do about it?" I asked. "We'll get back to you," was the response.

Well, surprisingly enough they did. The next day Sally called me. "When do you want your treatment?" she asked.

Being of a suspicious nature, I immediately asked, "What's this gonna cost me?" "Free," she said, and I immediately burst into song. A couple weeks later, two goons came out, drilled holes in my bathroom floor, and pumped chemicals down. Hooray, Hooray! Case closed, right? Wrong, life is never so simple.

Two weeks later, MW took me back downstairs—"Queenie" and her hordes were back, and seemed determined to make up for lost time. &%$*@!

Back on the phone the next day. Sally said she'd have someone out. A week passed — no visit — another call to Sally — this time with a nasty edge in my voice. Another inspector was out that day. "Yup," he said, "They're back. We screwed up and didn't drill the holes close enough together. We'll come back out and re-do it."

Well they did. This time, they poured enough poison to keep Dow Chemical busy for a week. "Queenie" and brood checked out, and did not return.

I later ran into my Realtor, who laughed when told the story. "Those inspections are just a formality, they probably do twenty a day. You're lucky. They must of figured you were gonna make trouble for 'em."

Believe me, I was. Making trouble is how you get the big payoff. I will discuss that further in the rest of the book. But first, a few pointers on phone call complaints:

a. **Don't lose your cool.** Although Charley Gumsmack was driving me up the wall with his pops, smacks, and various other sound effects, I maintained my air of sorrow and hurt. Getting into a shouting match with some oaf may do wonders for your ego, but probably not the old pocketbook. The name of the game was to save $640 smacks, not to exercise my tonsils.

b. **Get names.** Keep a record of who you talked to and what they said — you may need it for later.

c. Be prepared to write a letter. In this situation I got off easy — usually I've got to break out the old typewriter. But that will be discussed in the next chapter.

Final Results: "Queenie" wasted — house protected. Net savings: $640.

CHAPTER 2

THE COMPLAINT LETTER

Rent-a-Reque

In the first chapter I showed you an example of complaining over the phone. Frankly, I don't recommend that tactic. There's too good a chance you'll lose your "cool" and end up in an unproductive shouting match. But the most critical shortfall of telephones is (unless you're a Phone Phreak) you won't have any records of what actually went down over Ma Bell's little toy. Letters, however, are copyable (and you must copy everything that goes out and comes in), and will provide you with solid ammunition when you need it.

So on with the show . . .

While living in Washington State, Moi, MW, and the two crumb-snatchers decided to go on an Alaskan vacation. The day we left, I called EZ Go Rent-a-Car to have a car waiting at the airport. Well, naturally there was no car waiting at Anchorage when we landed. Cathy Carhop, trying to be helpful, offered me one of their "shuttle" cars at a reduced rate. It was late in the day and we were all tired, so I agreed.

Well, the car was filthy, but the beer cans under the seat (unfortunately empty) were of a brand I often drink, so off we drove. The fact it had standard shift precluded MW (being a Southern-bred Georgia Peach) from driving, but for a reason I will discuss later, I convinced her I would just drive the four days we were gonna spend in "The Last Frontier."

Driving to our motel, I noticed my pony was running hot. When we got there, I found her a quart low on oil, and the radiator only about half full. I made the appropriate additions (getting a receipt for the oil) and we retired for the night.

The next day was spent exploring Anchorage and environs. "Old Paint" still ran a little hot, but nothing that couldn't be handled by running the heater once in awhile. (As the weather was rainy and cool, we really didn't mind.)

The real fun began the next day. We had just left Anchorage heading up to Denali National Park to see Mt. McKinley (about 175 miles over "roads" that would have done Dan'l Boone proud) when the brake warning light came on. I called old EZ Go, and asked for another car. Can you guess their response? Right, no other cars available. "Bring it in to our garage near the airport, and we'll have a look."

About two hours later we were on the road again, the brake warning light still on. "It's still got some air in the lines, but it will go out after a few miles," said smiling Marty Mechanic. (It went out just before I turned it in, two days later.) By now, children, I was composing my complaint letter as we bounced our way to Denali.

The final buttstroke came when I turned my "Lil' Lemon" in. I had an EZ Go promotional coupon—rent four days and

pay for three. Cathy Carhop refused to honor it. "This looks
like a coupon for corporate renters only, sir." It was late at
night (we were going back on a Redeye special) so I paid the
$197.00 and left.

Within two days of returning home, I had my letter writ-
ten. I gave 'em both barrels, and included all my receipts
(copies, mind you, always keep the originals) and told 'em I'd
never use their scuzball cars again.

One minor problem — I decided to go right to the top and
write EZ Go's headquarters, figuring I'd get better results
from them — but I had no earthly idea where they were
hiding. A trip to the library (see Appendix III — Some Good
Sources) showed me EZ Go was owned by BigWig Holding
Company, out of Chicago. So that's where my letter went.

About three weeks later I got a letter from Gus Greasy,
Executive Vice/Assistant President for Something or Other of
BigWig, apologizing and promising a full investigation. "You
will be advised of the results," he oozed.

(Footnote from American History 101: In the late 1800's
a gentleman made a long trip on a railroad sleeper car. The
car had bedbugs, who tormented our hero the entire trip. He
wrote a scathing letter to the President of the Railroad, and
received a lengthy letter of apology, advising him the linens
in question had been burned and the entire railroad car fumi-
gated. They were so sorry and assured him this would never
happen again. Unfortunately, pinned to this letter was a
handwritten note — "Send this A--hole The Bedbug Letter.")

It's gratifying to note that the corporate standards of our
ancestors are just the same as today's. I waited another month
after hearing from Gus before deciding "The Windy City"
had blown me off with another "Bedbug Letter." So this
time two more letters went out (with copies of all previous
correspondence attached), one to the Better Business Bureau,
Anchorage, Alaska, and the other to the Alaskan Attorney

General's Office. ATTN: Consumer Protection, State Capital, Juneau, Alaska. I saw Gus's bluff and raised the ante.

The wheels continued to slowly grind. In two weeks my letter to the Better Business Bureau came back — addressee unknown — apparently Anchorage had no such organization. This is somewhat unusual, as most big cities in the United States do, so one arrow was wasted. But the other was not. Two more weeks passed before I heard from the Alaskan Attorney General — they were investigating my complaint. (I had gotten particularly nasty by now, in my letter I lamented that EZ Go had rented me an unsafe car, with bad brakes that could have killed Little Tommie and all the other mice, that my vacation was ruined, that I would never visit Alaska again [too true, too expensive up there for my cheapskate heart], etc., etc.)

Two more months passed (it was over Xmas, so I realized things would be slow). I was preparing another letter to both BigWig and the Alaskan Attorney General, when a letter came from EZ Go Anchorage. Enclosed was a check for $27.50 — one day's rent — "We're sorry our counter girl refused your coupon," they meekly said, "And hope this makes it up to you." "Well," sez I to MW, "not much, but will pay for a night on the town."

Imagine my surprise two days later when another EZ Go Alaska letter arrived. Enclosed was another humble pie letter to me, a copy of a letter to the Alaskan Attorney General saying EZ Go had done me right, plus a check for $197.00! A complete refund! Hell, I made $27.50 on the deal! (Less postage.)

OK, time out for some rules:

a. Always keep originals and send copies. If you don't have a copier where you work, try the local Post Office or Library. Office Supply and Print Shops often have copiers, too, but they are usually more expensive.

b. Give the company a reasonable time to handle your complaint. But beware of "Bedbug Letters" and be prepared to quickly escalate if you think you're getting the brush off.

c. Maintain a tone of hurt and sorrow, at least in your first letters—again you don't need to turn 'em off from the start. As time goes by, get nastier, talk about siccing your lawyer on them (even if the only lawyer you know is Raymond Burr from Perry Mason Re-runs), or "advising the appropriate government agencies." (Let them figure out what Agencies you're gonna complain to.) Hopefully, they'll decide you're not worth the cost of a lawsuit, or having some Government Agency breathing down their necks and will decide to buy you off. (Look at Appendix I for some sample letters.)

Final Results: A free rent a car and 27 bucks profit.

CHAPTER 3

FLY BY NITE
AIRLINES

The Trip To
Nowhere
and
The Squashed Baby
Stroller

I hate airlines. Big plastic buses with wings—escalators that fly. They cram you in like sardines, feed you inedible food, and let you wait for a bathroom built for pygmies. Then when you finally arrive at your destination—you wait an hour for luggage, that's often dinged up or lost. Yes, the Titmouse don't like airlines. But in the following two examples, he fought the "sky pirates" and won!

I was serving in West Germany with old US Army. Since the Titmice clan had emigrated from Ireland, Little Tommy decided to go look for "Roots". Me, MW, and little Titmouse #1 signed up with a famous tour agency (who nowadays deluge us with TV commercials starring a famous (?) actor)

to fly to "The Emerald Isle", spend a week, and fly back to
Nazi-land. Well, the tour went so-so—it was December, the
rainy season. The grass is so green there 'cause of all the rain
they get—and believe there was plenty of it. It was cold, too.
Titmouse Travel guide recommends you travel to Ireland in
the Spring/Summer!

But the fun was yet to begin. It was a Saturday night when
we returned to Dublin, went to the airport, and turned in our
rent-a-car. We went up to the counter and plopped down our
tickets for our night flight back to Sauerkraut, West Germany.
Can we guess what happened next, class? The flight ran 6
days (nights) a week. Guess what night it didn't run? Yeah,
German Mumbly Tours had booked us on a nonexistent
flight!

I was livid, but there wasn't a damn thing I could do. We
had two choices, spend the night in Dublin, and catch the
same flight the following night, or fly to London, spend the
night, and catch an early morning flight back to Schnitzel-
land (leaving at 6 in the morning—ugh!) We opted for the
latter—got to London late, spent about 5 hours (for $100)
sleeping at a hotel next to the London Airport (we all know
how expensive airport hotels are), and flew back to US Army,
Germany Sunday morning.

Well as you can imagine, Titmouse was hot—no flight, and
all the extra expense of one more day on the road. I wrote
a blistering letter to German Mumbly, accusing them of
the highest level of incompetence. I detailed all my extra
expenses, and threw in a few extra—a phone call from Lon-
don to West Germany, and extra day's boarding of the TM's
cats at the kennel (Our neighbors had kept them for free),
and told German Mumbly they had cost me $250.

A week or so later I got my response—a groveling letter
from German Mumbly and a check for $250 — $125 of
which was profit. It pays to advertise!

My wife (MW) had another unfortunate experience on an airline. This came down again while we were in Germany. I had sent her and little Titmouse #1 to show off to the grandparents. LT#1 was about 9 months old, and did most of her traveling in a stroller. Landing at Frankfurt, Germany, they rode a shuttle bus from the plane to the terminal. The bus driver closed the door on LT#1 and the stroller. LT#1 wasn't hurt, but the stroller was DOA. The "stew" told MW to submit a claim for damaged baggage. Well, the folks at the baggage claim told MW to go pound sand. "Ve only deel vit baggage hier, zo zorry your stroller iss kaput!"

Luckily, I met MW at the airport, so LT#1 didn't have to be carried too far. I had to go to the library to get an address, as MW flew on a foreign airline, but in a couple weeks I had another masterpiece in the mail. The $15 stroller was up to $85, I was never gonna fly that airline again, and I was gonna tell all my fellow soldiers not to fly them, too! I crossed my fingers and waited.

This one took about a month, but I got my $85 check (a $75 profit) and a poorly written letter in garbled English telling me how sorry "Sieg Heil" Airlines was, and would I please give them another try. To tell the truth, we left D-land shortly thereafter, and I never did fly "Sieg Heil". I hope they're not waiting on me!

The moral of this chapter then is this—never be afraid to complain, especially when you've been screwed by some blundering dolt (like the stew and the travel agent), who give you wrong information. Most major corporations have a "slush fund" for taking care of disgruntled customers. They want you to shut up and avoid giving them any bad publicity —so go for it!

CHAPTER 4

BATTLE OF THE BANK

The Bogus Withdrawal

The Titmouse don't care too much for banks, either. They always seem ready to take your money (as long as it makes the minimum deposit), but often reluctant to give it back. Make a small error in your checking account, and they're liable to come after you faster than Mad Mothers go after Drunk Drivers. Yet when they make mistakes . . .

Somewhere in Germany, West. The Titmouse is there, defending you, your Aunt Mildred, and that girl who used to give you hickeys at the Drive-In. The first indication that something was wrong took place when MW got a call that she had bounced a check at the local Commissary (Army version of Safeway for all you non-military types.) "How can this be?'' sez I. "We still got money in the bank." Well the next few days were a nightmare—letters, phonecalls—all demanding repayment (plus $10-$15) for checks returned for "insufficient funds". Luckily, I had another account to draw upon, but I was mighty confused.

Soon thereafter, I got my monthly bank statement from Hold'emup Bank, Inc. There amongst all the checks was a little blue slip—authorized deduction—$234. What the hell was this? I immediately called the bank from my home phone. The girl was nice, admitted it was a mistake and said I'd get the money back. That was swell, but a few days later I posted a letter to the Bank President. I thanked him for his helpful people, then lowered the boom. I reminded him I had spent $100 for a long distance phone call from Germany to the USA to straighten out the problem (actually it was about $50) plus $15 a pop (some were only $10, but what the heck) for each of the several checks his minions had played handball with. I threw in a little bit about being a poor "serviceman overseas protecting our American way of life", and then threw the spitball. I casually mentioned I was thinking about writing the Federal Reserve Board and the Federal Trade Commission to complain. As a final kick in the groin, I said I had decided to close my account "after so many years", and that I intended to tell my fellow soldiers how crummy his bank was. I sat back and waited for the firestorm.

Sure enough, a couple weeks later I got a nice letter from one Vice President/Flunky of the bank. He apologized profusely, begged me to stay with the bank, and advised me they had credited my account the $100 for the phone call, plus all the "$15" fees I had mentioned. I had won another one.

I learned later from a buddy that banks hate to have either the Federal Trade Commission or Federal Reserve in their knickers. He also advised me that State Attorney Generals

can also bring great smoke upon banks. So don't be intimi-
dated, even when you're 3,000 miles away, you can still make
the plutocrats sweat. All power to the People! (And their
Underwoods!)

CHAPTER 5

MAIL ORDER
MADNESS

Counterfeit Coins
and
Rusty Helmets

I have two hobbies that keep me occupied (and sometimes in trouble—MW says I have two hobbies too many!) One is coin collecting, the other Militaria, specifically, collecting old military helmets. I've had to do battle over both on several occasions. Two examples follow . . .

Anytime you buy items through the mail, the Federal Trade Commission says you can return for a refund if not satisfied. Some folks seem to want to forget this. It sometimes takes a two by four to remind them.

I had ordered two coins from a dealer who I had never done business with before. The prices were a bargain (which should have warned me) but I sent the money off anyway. It was to prove to be a mistake.

When the coins came I was disgusted. One looked to be counterfeit, while the other, although genuine, had been harshly cleaned (looked like with a Brillo pad) and was covered with nicks, scratches, and cuts. I immediately sent them back (the very next day) with a letter saying I wasn't satisfied with their condition and asking for my money back.

About two weeks later I got a package back. Inside was another coin—something I hadn't ordered at all! He said he was sorry I didn't like the first two, and offered to trade for the new coin he had sent.

Although I hadn't ordered this coin, it was a lot nicer (and more valuable) than the two I had returned. In fact it was much more valuable—if genuine. A little alarm went off in my head—first he hadn't sent me the money, second, he had sent me a very rare coin instead. "Mouse", I said to myself, "There ain't no Santa Claus. This guy is a crook." I immediately returned it, telling him thanks, but I wanted my money back. (I also had someone else look at the second coin— "bogus" was the verdict.)

Imagine my surprise when in a couple more weeks he sent me the same first two coins again! This was war! The coins were in the mail back to him that afternoon. The next day letters went out to the US Postal Inspector of his city, the Better Business Bureau of his city (I just guessed they had one), and the Attorney General of his state. In each letter I outlined my problem with the coin dealer, and asked for their help.

Within a month I had heard from all three of the above, telling me they were investigating. Within 6 weeks I had my money back. Later (about a year), I saw in one of my coin magazines that this same dealer had been sent to prison by the local Postal Investigators. He had been convicted of selling counterfeit and altered coins, and of cheating people out of millions of dollars in refunds for coins they had returned!

I was amazed (and lucky, too). I had gotten my money back —$240, but I must have been one of the few. I like to think that perhaps my letter to the Postal Inspector helped put this guy away. My suspicions had been true. He was a crook! The only way I figure it out is 'cause I complained to everybody in sight, he decided to shut me up by sending me my money back. I guess the others he cheated didn't yell loud enough, or maybe by the end he just didn't send anyone any money back.

I have a nice collection of old Military helmets in my den, going to WWI (the big one your grandfather fought in.) None are particularly rare, but they give the room a nice neo-fascist look. I had been looking for several years for a Bulgarian WWII helmet. They had fought alongside the Nazis against Russia on the Eastern Front, so not too many of the helmets (or Bulgarian soldiers) had survived!

I got a list from a dealer who said he could get almost anything. I wrote and asked about a Bulgarian helmet. He wrote back shortly saying he had one, at a very good price. (When will I ever learn about "bargains"!) I sent him a check. After 6 weeks nothing—the check had cleared, so I wrote him— where is my helmet? He wrote back it was shipped the day after he got my check—lost in the mail—he'd find out what "and get back to you ASAP". Well, after a month I called. "It's lost," he said, "I don't have another one right now, but once I get the money from the insurance, I'm sure I can turn up another." "OK," said the Mouse, "Go for it!"

Another month passed. A box came by UPS to the house. Excitedly I ripped it open to find a rusty German WWII helmet—not what I had ordered at all. I sent it back with a letter saying that was not what I wanted and to please refund my money. Another month, another package came. Inside I found a Greek helmet from the 1960's! This time I blew a cork. I sent him the helmet back, with a little note—money back in two weeks or I write Federal Trade Commission, Postal Inspector, Better Business Bureau, and State Attorney General. In a week MW got a call—he was madder than a pistol and demanded I call him. I didn't, but a week later I got my money back. Naturally, I've never done business with him again—and he is now out of business. It took me a few months, but chalk up another victory for the Titmouse.

Anyway, dear reader, here's the scoop. **Don't be satisfied with mail order trash you get through the mail. If it's not what you want or ordered, send it back. If the merchant gets tough, get the address of his local Postal Inspector from your Post Office and drop them a line. State Attorney Generals and local Better Business Bureaus can also be helpful. Many big cities (New York, Philadelphia, etc.) have their own Consumer Protection Boards—just write the Mayor—one of his staff will get it to the right office. The point is, don't ever give up—complain loud and long and often. Get your money back!**

CHAPTER 6

THE LARCENOUS LANDLORD

The Unreturned Deposit

I was living in the "Evergreen State", Washington, when I had to make a fast cross-country move to where I'm living now. I was renting a house, so I wrote my landlady about a month in advance to let her know I was moving out. (I wrote her for two reasons—first I wanted to be able to prove I had given her 30 days notice, and second she had an unlisted phone number!) She called me within a few days and told me she would be out of town while I was moving. (She was not the owner of the house, just a Realtor acting as a Rental Agent.) We agreed I would turn the key over to my neighbor, who would then pass it on to her. I gave her a forwarding address, and bid her farewell.

Now, before I go on with this tale, I may as well tell you that the deposit was only $150. When I moved in, the place was a pigpen. The lawn looked like a Brazilian Rain Forest, and there was enough mold in the fridge to make a year's supply of penicillin (plus the damn refrigerator door fell off when I opened it!)

Anyhow, me and MW had cleaned the place up pretty well by the time the Titmice moved out of there. After a couple weeks of no check, I dropped her a line—no answer. I waited a couple more weeks and tried again, this time with a certified letter. When this brought no effect, I started my retaliatory strikes. Letters went out to the Attorney General, State of Washington and the Consumer Protection Bureau, care of the Mayor of the city where she lived. (Again, I just assumed a big city would have some type of Agency to handle complaints against landlords/businesses, etc.)

Soon I started getting answers in the mail—but not good ones. The certified letter came back—she had moved and the letter was never claimed. Luckily, the Post Office had put her new address on the envelope, so I wrote her at that address. I also called the information operator, but she still had an unlisted number, even at the new address.

My letters to the Attorney General and the Mayor were disappointments. They both answered me, telling that it was out of their hands due to some bogus court ruling and that I needed to sue her in State of Washington Small Claims Court. Seeing as how I was sitting in the State of Maryland, that idea was not very attractive. Hell, the plane fare was more than she owed me! Plus with a new job, I didn't think my boss was too hot on me taking a couple week's leave to hash this one out.

I was desperate. She had ripped me off and I wasn't gonna let her get away with it! By now about two months had passed. What's a boy (mouse) to do? One night, mulling over this great injustice, a flash of insight hit me like a tidal wave. She was a Realtor! Realtors are licensed by the state they do business in! The next day a letter went out to the Washington State Realty Commission, Olympia, Washington. (I wasn't sure of the exact name, but I figured if I sent it to the State Capital, it would eventually hit the right desk.)

A month later I got my money back. She claimed she had lost my address. Funny thing, I never heard a peep from the Realty Commission. Coincidence? I really don't know. But I do know I got my money back, and that, boys and girls, is the bottom line!

The points I hope you get from this chapter are these— **Don't** give up and always continue to look for leverage. I didn't get it with the Mayor or the Attorney General, but I think the Realty Commission put me over the top. Doctors, lawyers, dentists, and even exterminators are licensed by the State/County where they operate. Often they belong to professional organizations (See Appendix II) that you can complain to. You want to make their life unbearable, so they'll give you the money back. I had one fellow beg me to call off the hounds after he had written me an insulting letter and defied me to get my money back, and I therefore had written a few letters of my own. This raises another point—always be gracious in your victories. When you get your money back (and always wait a few days on checks to clear), send a 14-cent postcard to all the offices you complained to and tell them the issue is settled. It's only fair to tidy up the battlefield after you chased the enemy from the field.

I didn't make any money on this little escapade, and postage costs were a couple dollars—but $125 sounds better in the old wallet than $000!

CHAPTER 7

AUTOMOBILE DEALS

Tired Tires
and
Bad Batteries

Warranties are often hard to enforce, especially when one is 2,000 miles away. But the following two stories, dealing with problems I had with my car, will hopefully show you that all is not lost when stuff breaks far away from the dealer who sold it to ya. Again, it's the squeaky wheel that gets the grease!

Winter of 1982, I was living in the DC area, and MW was expecting little Titmouse #2. The hospital was about a 30 minute drive from the house. Those of you familiar with the DC area no doubt know that winters there are unpredictable. LT#2 was due 28 February, so I didn't want any foul-ups. My car at that time was an AMC Hornet Station Wagon (still

have it today, 136,000+ miles and still rolling along!), in
pretty good shape but the tires were getting a little slick. I
started watching the paper for sales . . .

Cheap Charlie's Discount Tires had a special on Radial
Retreads, All Season, with a 20,000 mile warranty. The price
was good, too damn good, as I was to find out. I went down
and bought four new tires.

LT#2 was late, coming on 5 March. Me and MW had a
midnight ride, but no problems—it did snow pretty good a
couple days later, but by then LT#2 had already arrived. No
problems on the tires, yet . . .

The fun started in June. The Titmice were driving down to
Georgia to see the in-laws on I95. We had just crossed the
North Carolina State line when we heard a horrible banging.
I stopped and checked it out. A piece of the tire had peeled
off and was beating against the wheel well. I was completely
flabbergasted! We bought a new tire and I threw the old one
on the roof. Imagine my surprise a few more miles down the
road when another one blew—just disintegrated off the rim. I
limped into another station.

As they put on my second new tire of the day, I talked to
the owner of the station. He told me that recapping radial
tires was very difficult and more often than not, didn't work.
He felt the heat of the prolonged driving on the Interstate
caused them to self-destruct. I was ready to believe him.

We got to Georgia a day late. Immediately I went to an-
other tire store and had the other two retreads pulled off and
replaced. I now had four extra tires, all tied down on the roof
of the car. I pulled out my warranty from the glove compart-
ment and called Cheap Charlie's Corporate Headquarters.

I was 800+ miles away, I explained to the man what had
happened, that two tires had died on me, and I had replaced
the others, for fear of their going bad, too. To my surprise,
he was very nice—"Just bring them back for a full refund,"

he said. I did—and they gave me my money back, plus an apology! I noticed shortly thereafter Cheap Charlie's stopped running ads for those retreads. Something tells me I wasn't the only one who had trouble with those tires. All's well that ends well I guess—LT#2 arrived safely, I used those tires for three months and I got my money back in the end.

Right before I left DC for Washington State, I bought a new battery for the car. It wasn't a "name brand" but it had a 42-month warranty—the only problem was, the store I bought it from didn't have stores in Washington State. I guess you can figure out what happened—Yup it died after a few months and I had to get a new battery. I had saved the warranty paperwork, however, and wrote the store a letter. In it I explained I had moved cross country, and it was a little hard to bring them the battery back for replacement. I enclosed a copy of the warranty and of the bill for a new battery. In a couple of weeks I got a refund check from the store and a letter of apology. I had won another one!

I must admit to you that the above two examples were the easiest refunds I ever got. Kinda restored my faith in American Business, too (well, at least those two companies). I was miles away from where I had purchased the items, but both companies were big enough to admit their mistakes and refund my money. No hassles, no BS, no trying to weasel out. They sent me the money and apologized. Too bad everybody doesn't do business that way. (But if that was the case, I would never have written this book—and you wouldn't be reading it!)

One final note, if they had given me a hard time, I would have immediately escalated the battle. The Virginia Attorney General and the DC Consumer Protection Bureaus would have been notified. If that still had brought no results, the Federal Trade Commission and the Traffic Safety Foundation would have been notified (after all, dissolving tires are dangerous, right?). Like I told you in the last chapter—BEAT 'EM TILL THEY BLEED!

CHAPTER 8

CREDIT CARD FOLLIES

Over-Payment Blues

Credit cards are strange animals. Like a genie they can take you to far away places—Japan, Hawaii, Europe, etc. They can also take you to the poorhouse! I'll now relate a couple of my battles with credit card companies, for your personal enjoyment and amusement.

I was still in the Army, just back from Germany. I found myself in Arizona, Ft. Huachuca, to be exact, about 70 miles southeast of Tucson. Mail was being forwarded from Germany, usually two weeks late, and we were frantically trying to pay the bills as they came in, before we got hit with a late or missed payment charge. At the same time, of course, we were giving them our new address.

To make a long story short, we somehow managed to pay one bill twice. I noticed the bill for a national department store showed $125.00CR when it came in. I drove off post into Sierra Vista, the one-horse burg next to the base. (Not really a bad town—it even had a small store of the chain I needed to talk to about the bill.)

I showed my bill to the young man at the credit department who confirmed my suspicions, that yes, we had overpaid the XXX Store by $125.00! "Well," sez I, "I'd like a refund." "No can do," he simpered, "Just go out and charge something for $125.00."

That was not what I had in mind. I argued briefly with the giggling moron, but soon realized it was hopeless. Naturally, his supervisor wasn't there. (Doesn't that always seem to be the case?) I gave up and left the store. But mind you, I wasn't finished yet. Indeed, I had not yet begun to fight as some famous American sailor once hollered.

Now XXX Store was a nationwide chain. I really wasn't too sure exactly where to write. So I resorted to trickery. The next day I called Customer Service at the local store, and spun them a yarn about one of their people being so kind and friendly and asking where the next higher head office was, so that I could write a nice letter. (You don't think I was gonna tell them the truth, do you—they probably would have never given me the address!) Well, they were tickled pink—and gave me the address up in Tucson. Gotcha!

The next day my letter went out. It was full of pathos and pain, how I, a poor soldier, just back from Germany defending "Our American Way of Life" had been cheated by XXX Store. I threw in a little zinger about "telling all my fellow soldiers how you treated me", sat back and waited. It didn't take long. Within a week, Ms. Smoothvoice called me—not only were they sending me my money back, but also a $25 gift certificate "for all your troubles". I used that to buy something later, which I exchanged for cash. So a cool $25 profit for a 22¢ stamp!

Credit card companies love you when you don't pay them off each month. That way the next month, they can charge you interest on "the average daily balance", which includes everything you charged the next month, too. I always try to pay them off to avoid this. So you can imagine my anger when I got a USACARD bill one month showing I had not paid the last month's bill by three cents, and hitting me with an interest charge.

Well, I dashed off another scathing letter, informing them I always paid my bills off each month, and who were they trying to kid. They never answered me, but the next bill showed a correction of 3¢, plus the interest they charged me. The funniest part about this is I was wrong! When I got my back statement back, I saw I had written the check for $xx.90, instead of $xx.93! But I guess they figured it wasn't worth fighting over, so they gave me the money back anyway. I wonder who had to cough up the 3¢? (No doubt it came out of their "slush fund" for silencing irate customers.)

Another good suggestion to keep in mind is always keep a record of what you charged. One time I got a bill that included $12.00 worth of another person's prescription drug purchases! A fast phone call fixed that up, no letter was needed. But unless you get your jollies playing Santa for somebody else's medicine, keep your eye on the charge card bills when they come in!

So there you have it. Charge cards can be challenged, too. Just remember one thing—most charge accounts insist you tell them of discrepancies in writing—a phone call won't cut the mustard. So if you think the old "Get in Debt Fast" Charge Card Company is doing ya dirty, don't be afraid to yell—but do it in writing.

CHAPTER 9

OVERSEAS EROTICA
Swedish Meatballs

I once sent a postal money order to a company in Sweden that specialized in books and magazines not usually found in your average American bookstore. (This was a few years ago when the local bluenoses kept us all safe from lust and perversion.) Sad to say, I no longer dabble in such delites, as MW took a dim view of my collection and made me trash same shortly after I made an honest woman of her. (But we're getting ahead of the story. So on with the show!)

After a couple of months of anxiously awaiting my films, I realized that the 8mms were not forthcoming. Another letter to the company brought no response. I realized I was dealing with a different situation from some of my previous attacks on ripoff artists. It took me awhile, but I finally found out how to get leverage on 'em (and my materials delivered!)

I went down to the local library. There I grabbed a Washington, DC phone book. (Many libraries carry out of state phone books, although sometimes you'll find them on microfiche, which is I admit, a pain but still they contain what you need.) I looked up the Embassy of Sweden, got their address, and wrote them a letter. In it, I explained I was doing some business with a company in their country that had done me wrong. (In this instance I didn't get specific on what I ordered, just enclosed a copy of the postal money order receipt and said the "materials" I ordered hadn't arrived. They probably figured out what was going on, but at least I was discreet!) The embassy sent me back a nice letter, thanking me for my inquiry, and advising me they would attempt to contact the company for me. About a month later a package from Sweden was in the mailbox, and that night me and some of my buddies had our film fest. I made some good money later on renting those films out to stag parties, but that's another story.

In the above example, it took me a few months to figure out a way to hammer "Swedish Meatballs, INC", but when I finally hit them, they coughed up—don't want any international incidents over skin flicks, right folks? The point is to never let up.

In another case I ordered a new magazine for my .45 automatic pistol from a company in California. They had the gall to cash my check and then tell me the wait was two months. (The Federal Trade Commission requires companies to advise you when merchandise is out of stock for more than 30 days, and to give you the option to cancel your order. These Bozos simply told me to wait for two months!)

After two months of waiting I wrote them to cancel my order and refund my money. They ignored me. I then called, but never could seem to talk to anybody except an order clerk (female type) who whimpered and pleaded ignorance. I started to go through my drill of writing the Postal Inspector and the State Attorney General, but decided instead to write to the magazine in which I saw their original ad. This worked like a charm. The magazine wrote me to say they'd check it out—shortly thereafter I got my refund check.

Now I must warn you, this doesn't always work. I have had other instances when magazines have blown me off. "We cannot police our advertisers. Sorry." So sometimes it's worth the postage, sometimes not. It's your nickel!

Professional Organizations are also sometimes good folks to complain to about problems you are having with members of their organization. The Direct Mail Marketing Association in New York City (See Appendix II) can often help you with mail order merchants. The American Numismatic Society has often helped me when I had problems with coin dealers. Check with your librarian, as most libraries will have a dictionary of associations. You'll be surprised (well, at least I was) over the various associations that exist—cement masons, chocolate manufacturers, exterminators, morticians, automobile repair, etc., etc., etc. Just look up what type of an operation you're dealing with and write that particular association. Better yet, check out the business—see if his ad/shop identifies him affiliated with some association—but even if it doesn't, write anyway—the more the merrier—and you might get lucky! Go for it!

Well, I hope you've learned a little bit more from this chapter about dealing with mail order companies. They rely on volume business and your good will to make a profit. If you raise enough stink, they'll pay you off—usually. In the next chapter I'll talk about my one failure. (Hey! Even Babe Ruth struck out a few times ya know!)

CHAPTER 10

THE ONE THAT GOT AWAY

I cannot lie to you. I have given you examples of my victories. I must now tell you of my one defeat. As I told you previously, even Babe Ruth struck out once in awhile!

This story involves coins, specifically United States Mint Proof Sets, special sets of cent through half coins double struck from highly polished dies, and housed in a special holder. Each year the mint strikes these sets for sale to coin collectors. If one doesn't buy them from the mint during the year they are issued, the only option is to buy them from a dealer, who will charge you a premium. Older sets (1930's-40's) are quite valuable, some, like the 1936 set, costing thousands of dollars!

Well, I didn't order a 1936 set, but I ordered some sets in the 1960's from a coin dealer's ad in a nationally known coin publication. They were to be a present for my Mom (Mother Titmouse), who also collects coins.

When the proof sets didn't arrive after a couple of weeks, I dropped the fellow a line inquiring as to the status of my order. I enclosed a copy of the Postal Money Order I had used to pay for them. I still received no response.

After this took place I went into my letter writing mode. I wrote the State Attorney General (in this case, Florida), the Jacksonville, Florida Postal Inspector (since this was the nearest big city), the Jacksonville Better Business Bureau, the American Numismatic Association, and the coin publication I saw the ad in.

Over the next few weeks I heard from all those folks. He turned out to not belong to the American Numismatic Association and the Jacksonville Better Business Bureau said he wasn't in their jurisdiction. All the other folks said they'd investigate my claim and get back to me. I ended up waiting quite awhile. Several follow-up letters just brought "we're still working on it" type responses. The coin magazine finally gave up and told me to contact the Jacksonville Postal Inspector (which, of course, I already had!)

It was almost a year later that I finally got a letter from the Postal Authorities which resolved the matter (but not in my favor, I'm afraid). They advised me that my adversary had been sentenced to prison for mail fraud, for taking orders for several thousand dollars worth of coins and delivering zip to many folks, myself included. The letter also advised me that the sentencing did not include provisions for restitution to the victims. So there I was—out $12.00 and a couple dollars for postage. For a long time I kept my copy of the Postal Money Order Receipt, but I finally threw that away, too. It was a souvenir I decided not to keep—who wants to remember their defeats, anyway!

So there you have it. I went through all the right moves, but still ended up flat. I just want to tell you this to remind you that even the best of us don't always get our money back. But that doesn't mean you quit! It just means to go after the next Bozo who tries to stiff you even harder!

CHAPTER 11

FINAL HINTS

I have tried to give you some examples on how to fight back when you've been burned by some knucklehead who thinks he can walk over you without a fight. Every one of the stories I told you is true—these situations actually happened to Tom Titmouse and the Titmice family. In some instances, I blurred details a bit, just to protect the guilty, but other than that everything came down just the way I told you.

I'd like to end this little manuscript with three final words of advice—if you can remember these three little words— you'll come out ok in the end (and most likely get your money back!)

Patience—don't lose your cool. Always contact the merchant/landlord/whatever first. Speak calmly and correctly (even if you have the urge to kill), explaining the problem and ask them to correct the situation. Make a note of to whom you talked, what they told you, and the date/time. When this fails (as sadly, it too often does), write your letters. Make copies of all bills/receipts and enclose copies. Here again you must be patient—don't expect the Better Business Bureau to be on your doorstep the next morning—these cases take time and there are many complaints and few investigators. (I usually give 'em a month—if I get no response by then, I write another letter.)

Perseverance—You gotta hang tough. As I said in my chapter on Swedish Meatballs, you have to get leverage. Sometimes a letter to the home office of a big corporation gets results. Sometimes you can bring heat on them through the federal, state, or county governments. I have never used them, but some big city newspapers have "Troubleshooter"-consumer advocate columnists who will chase these boobs down for you. So keep writing, keep squeaking and squawking—the more noise you make, the better are the chances you'll get paid off to shut up.

Postage—it takes money to make money. Send letters to everyone you think could help you. Hell, I've written Mayors, Governors, State Attorney Generals, Ambassadors, and Presidents of Banks, Corporations, etc. Send the letters certified and/or registered—but send them. Show them you mean business.

There you have it. I've put down on paper enough tips/examples that should carry you through any battle you wish to start. It isn't always easy, and I cannot swear you'll always win, but as far as I'm concerned, the bottom line is "green"—and if you fight long and hard enough—that's what will be in your pocket, instead of some lout's who took you for an easy mark! Good luck to you—now go get 'em tiger!

APPENDIX I

SOME SAMPLE LETTERS

In the next few pages I will present sample letters based upon three actual cases in my never ending struggles for truth, justice, and the American way. The first group deals with my struggle with a coin dealer in New York City who tried to stick me with a counterfeit coin. He started out real nasty, but by the time I was through with him, he was begging me to call off the hounds. You can use letters like these whenever you are dealing with mail order dealers. The second set deals with my fight to get my security deposit back from a recalcitrant rental agent. I got my check in three weeks after writing the last set of letters. The final set involves my actions taken against my bank, when they bounced a check on me, despite the fact there was money in the account. I got some-one fired for this.

The main points I want you to get from these letters are the following:

Always be nice, each letter should be written "more in sorrow than in anger." You can get a little nastier as time goes by, but keep it clean and never get too insulting.

"Just the facts," as the old TV Cop used to say. Keep your letter simple and direct, explain your problem as simply as you can, and then ask for help in solving the prob-lem.

Send copies of invoices, bills, receipts for regis-tered/insured packages, and any letters you have sent to your antagonist. You want to be able to show you have tried to solve the problem, have failed, and now need outside help.

In short, use the following examples, to write your own "poison pen" letters, and get your money back from the SOBs!

12 Wart Lane
Firm, La 78909
1 July 1984

XXXXX Coin
XXXXXXXXXX
NY, NY 10049

Dear Sir:

Two weeks ago I returned to you via insured mail the 1907 50¢ Liberty coin you sold me. I was not satisfied with the condition and wish to receive my money back. I have heard nothing from you. Please expedite my refund. If the coin has not been received by you, please advise ASAP. Thanks.

T. Titmouse

12 Wart Lane
Firm, La 78909
14 July 1984

XXXXX Coin
XXXXXXXXXX
NY, NY 10049

Dear Sir:

Two weeks ago I wrote to you concerning the coin I had returned to you for refund. You have still not responded. If I do not receive my money within 10 days, I shall contact my attorney and take whatever actions are necessary to recover my money. Thank you.

T. Titmouse

Note: I have gotten a little nastier with this letter, but I am still giving him the benefit of the doubt, as the United States Postal Service has been known to lose letters. I do not actually have an attorney, but XXX Coin does not know that!

12 Wart Lane
Firm, La 78909
25 July 1984

(See Note Below for where I sent this letter.)

Dear Sir:

   I am requesting your assistance in my dealings with XXXXX Coin, XXXXXXXX, NY, NY 10049. Over a month ago I returned a coin purchased from him for refund. To date, despite several letters, I have heard nothing from him. I am enclosing copies of my letters and the postal insurance receipt for the package. I would appreciate any help you could give me in resolving this matter. Thank you for your help.

T. Titmouse

Note: This letter went to the following people: (I got most of the addresses out of the Zip Code Directory, looking under NYC Government Agencies!)

Chief Postal Inspector
NY, NY 10001

City of New York
Dpt of Consumer Affairs
80 Lafayette St.
NY, NY 10013

Better Business Bureau
NY, NY 10001
(I did not have an exact address for NY BBB, but sent it to
the General Delivery Zip Code—and they got it!)

City of New York
District Attorney
155 Leonard St.
NY, NY
10013

New York State Attorney General
Dept. of Consumer Affairs
Albany, NY 12207
(Guessed on this address, too.)

I had my money back in three weeks!

12 Wart Lane
Firm, La 78909
1 Jan. 1984

Ms. Wanda Witch
XXXXXXXXX
Tacoma, Wa 98406

Dear Ms. Witch:

It has been over three weeks since I moved out of the house I was renting from you. I would appreciate a prompt refund of my security deposit. Thank you.

T. Titmouse

Note: I had moved out while Ms. Witch was out of town. I had talked to her by phone and she told me to leave the key with a neighbor and she would mail me my deposit.

12 Wart Lane
Firm, La 78909
15 Jan. 1984

Ms. Wanda Witch
XXXXXXXXX
Tacoma, Wa 98406

Dear Ms. Witch:

It has been two weeks now since I wrote you asking about the return of my security deposit. You have failed to respond. If I do not receive my money within ten days I shall take whatever actions necessary (to include taking you to court) to get it back. Thank you.

T. Titmouse

Note: I sent this one certified mail with a return receipt, so I could prove she had gotten it. Taking her to court is really a bogus threat, as I was too far away to do so. (But she did not know that.)

12 Wart Lane
Firm, La 78909
25 Jan. 1984

(See Note Below)

Dear Sir:

I am asking for your help in my dealings with Ms. W. Witch, a Realtor who lives at XXXXXXX, Tacoma, Wa 98406. I rented a house at XXXXXXX, Tacoma, with Ms. Witch acting as the Rental Agent for the owner. I moved out in December, 1983. Ms. Witch was out of town, so acting on her telephonic instructions, I left the key with a neighbor. She promised she would send me my Security Deposit to my new (above) address. I have written her twice (copies of letters enclosed), but have heard nothing. I would appreciate any help you can give me in the matter. Thank you.

T. Titmouse

Note: This "loveletter" went out to:

Attorney General
State of Washington
Olympia, Wa 98503

Mayor
Attn: Consumer Protection Division
Tacoma, Wa 98406
(another "shot in the dark" that hit home)

State Realty Board
Attn: Consumer Complaints
Olympia, Wa 98503
(I figured since she was a licensed Realtor to send this letter
out "in the blind.")

It took a month, but I got my check. I think it was the letter
to the Realty Commissioners that pried it loose.

12 Wart Lane
Firm, La 78909
29 Feb. 1984

President
Grinch National Bank
XXXXXX, XXXXX 00000

Dear Sir:

I am enclosing a form letter I received from your bank today, advising me they had refused payment on 15 Feb. on a check for $42.50, citing "no funds available". I am also enclosing a deposit slip, also dated 15 Feb., for $150.00! In short, the money was present to cover the check. To add insult to injury, you also deducted $15.00 from my account. I have been checking at your bank for 10 years now, and I have never been treated so badly. If this is the way you handle your customers, I intend to take my business elsewhere!

T. Titmouse

Note: I got a nice "Bedbug Letter" from the bank, plus my $15.00 back. I heard later somebody got canned over this (and other) incidents. If this letter had had no effect, my next one would have been to the Federal Reserve Board, Washington, DC. The Fed is the "Watchdog" of the banking industry and a letter to them is sure to stir things up a bit.

APPENDIX II

AGENCIES
TO
CONTACT

Some addresses of people who can help. Note: I have put the addresses of the National Headquarters of several organizations—a call or letter to them can usually put you in touch with a local branch. I've also included addresses of some Professional Associations that might come in handy. So look down the list till you find someone dealing with the area you're having a problem with, and write/call. Even if they cannot help, they can often point you to someone who can!

Council of Better Business Bureaus
1515 Wilson Blvd.
Arlington, Va 22209 (703) 276-0100

Direct Mail Marketing Association
6 East 43rd St.
NY, NY 10017

Chief Postal Inspector
United States Postal Service
Washington, DC 20260 (202) 245-5445

Federal Trade Commission
6th and Pa Ave. NW
Washington, DC 20580 (202) 523-3567

Funeral Service Consumer Action Program
135 West Wells St.
Milwaukee, Wi 53203

Major Appliance Consumer Action Panel
20 North Wacker Dr.
Chicago, Ill 60606 (312) 984-5858   (800) 621-0477

Consumer Arbitration Center
National Association of Securities Dealers, Inc.
Two World Trade Center South Tower
98th Floor
NY, NY 10048 (212) 839-6200

Health Insurance Association of America
1850 K Street NW
Washington, DC 20006 (202) 862-4806   (800) 423-8000

Director, Consumer Affairs
Insurance Information Institute
110 Williams St.
NY, NY 10038 (212) 669-9200   (800) 221-4954

Director, Consumer Affairs/Public Liaison
National Association of Home Builders
15th and M St. NW
Washington, DC 20005 (202) 822-0409

National Association of the Remodeling Industry
11 East 44th St.
NY, NY 10017 (212) 867-0121

Director, Public Policy
National Council of Health Centers
2600 Virginia Av. NW
Suite 1100
Washington, DC 20037 (202) 298-7393

National Foundation for Consumer Credit
8701 Georgia Av.
Suite 601
Silver Spring, Md 20910 (301) 589-5600

National Tire Dealers and Retreaders Association
1250 Eye St. NW
Washington, DC 20009 (202) 234-5100

Pharmaceutical Manufacturers Association
1100 15th St. NW
Suite 900
Washington, DC 20005 (202) 835-3468

Public Information Manager
Toy Manufacturers of America
200 Fifth Av.
NY, NY 10010 (212) 675-1141

Attorney General
Your State Capital, Your State
(Look in the Postal Service Zip Code Directory for zip codes
of State Buildings in your State Capital.)

Insurance Commissioner*
Your State Capital, Your State

Chairman*
Public Utilities Commission
Your State Capital, Your State

Chairman*
Board of Realtor Licensing/Realty Commission
Your State Capital, Your State

Office of Public Affairs and Consumer Participation (NOA-42)
National Highway Traffic Safety Administration
Department of Transportation
Washington, DC 20590 (202) 426-0670

National Transportation Safety Board
800 Independence Av. SW
Washington, DC 20594 (202) 382-6606

Veterans Assistance Service
Veterans Administration
Washington, DC 20420 (202) 389-2567

Office of Consumer Affairs
Room 575
Department of Commerce
Washington, DC 20230 (202) 377-5001

National Administrator
Automotive Consumer Action Program (AUTOCAP)
9400 Westpark Dr.
McLean, Va 22102 (703) 821-7000

American Automobile Association
8111 Gatehouse Rd.
Falls Church, Va 22047 (703) 222-6000

Household Goods Dispute Settlement Program
400 Army Navy Dr.
Arlington, Va 22202 (703) 521-1111

Direct Selling Association
1730 M St. NW
Washington, DC 20036 (202) 293-5760

* These offices have different names in different states, but if you send them as I have shown, they should get to the right people eventually.

OTHER AVAILABLE TITLES